Original title:
Living with Passion

Copyright © 2024 Swan Charm
All rights reserved.

Editor: Jessica Elisabeth Luik
Author: Luise Luik
ISBN HARDBACK: 978-9916-86-244-5
ISBN PAPERBACK: 978-9916-86-245-2

Zeal Uncontained

In a forest of dreams, paths intertwined,
Where whispers of hope endlessly chime.
With every heartbeat, promises gained,
Fuel the fire of zeal uncontained.

Mountains echo tales of the brave,
Rivers carve freedom in every wave.
Stars align to guide the refrained,
Lighting the path of zeal uncontained.

Shadows falter, the dawn reclaims,
Daylight spreads through ancient veins.
With each sunrise, new strengths attained,
Mark the journey of zeal uncontained.

Ignite the Soul

A spark ignites in the twilight's glow,
Awakens dreams in silent flow.
The heart responds to the call of role,
Embrace the light, ignite the soul.

Through winds of change and tides so bold,
Stories of timeless grace unfold.
In whispered moments, secrets told,
Lift your spirit, ignite the soul.

Bound by neither time nor space,
Chase the echoes of an endless race.
Feel the fire, make the whole,
With passion pure, ignite the soul.

Searing Desires

In the night where shadows sleep,
Dreams of longing often creep.
Stars above with fervent gaze,
Burning bright, in endless blaze.

Heartbeats echo with delight,
In the silence of the night.
Whispers soft across the skies,
Searing pain, as love then flies.

Wishes cast upon the air,
In the hope that hearts will dare.
To the depth of ardor's fire,
Searing deep, the lost desire.

Passionate Pulse

Beneath the moon's soft silver shine,
Lovers' hearts begin to pine.
In the dance of life and time,
Passionate pulse, pure and prime.

Eyes that meet with blazing heat,
Echo heartbeats, wild and fleet.
In each touch, a spark ignites,
Flames that light the darkest nights.

Souls entwined in ardent plea,
Boundless shores of passion's sea.
Timeless rhythm, love's own drum,
Passionate pulse, where dreams come from.

Heart's Inferno

A blaze within, a wild embrace,
In every heart, a secret place.
Fiery trails that never cease,
Yearning for that sweet release.

Eyes of embers, soul of flame,
Burning bright, without a name.
Torrid whispers, shadows cast,
Heart's inferno, wild and vast.

Love's own forge, so fierce and grand,
Scorching seas of searing sand.
In the tempest, hearts will find,
Inferno's kiss, forever bind.

Wings of Flame

In the twilight's gentle hues,
Wings of flame begin to cruise.
Soaring high on winds of fate,
Towards the heavens, hearts elate.

Burning bright with fervent glow,
Passions' wings take flight and flow.
In the realm where dreams reside,
Wings of flame, hearts opened wide.

Echoes of a fire's tale,
Through the skies they light the trail.
Boundless love, no chains restrain,
Wings of flame, forever reign.

Radiant Pursuits

In the dawn of dreams we chase,
golden threads of morning light.
Hearts aglow, a steadfast pace,
through the embered wings of night.

Mountains whisper tales untold,
valleys echo our desires.
We pursue horizons bold,
fanned by passion's glowing fires.

Rivers carve our journey's way,
guiding us with liquid grace.
From the dusk to break of day,
hope ignites each seeking face.

Devotion in Motion

Waves crash on the yearning shore,
whispers of love deeply sown.
Every pulse, a call for more,
where devotion seeds are grown.

Windswept skies and stars align,
as we dance in twilight's gleam.
Hearts are bound in rhythmic sign,
swirled within a shared dream.

Through the trials, through the tears,
devotion's path remains clear.
In each step that time reveres,
together, we conquer fear.

Wild Heartbeats

Thunder roars in fields of green,
wild heartbeats that never cease.
In each glance, a world unseen,
where the untamed find their peace.

Footsteps echo on the ground,
trails of stories left behind.
In the wild, where love is found,
untamed spirits freely bind.

Fires spark beneath the moon,
casting shadows, dancing free.
Hearts that call a wild tune,
find their place in destiny.

The Flame Within

Embers glow in twilight's shroud,
silent whispers of the night.
In the heart so fierce and proud,
burns a flame, intensely bright.

Whispers turn to roaring blaze,
lighting paths through darkened skies.
Flames endure in endless ways,
in every tear, a strength lies.

Passion fuels the inner spark,
guiding us through trials grim.
Even in the deepest dark,
shines the flame, a guiding hymn.

Verve and Valor

Upon the winds of morning dew,
Strength and courage both renew,
Hearts of fire, minds of steel,
In the fight, we dare to feel.

Never yielding, always true,
Life's great storms we shall pursue,
In our veins, a fervent flame,
Bold and bright, we claim our name.

Through the shadows, through the fray,
Guided by a brighter day,
In the end, we soar and rise,
With verve and valor as our prize.

Blaze of Will

Through the night, our spirits soar,
Driven by an endless roar,
In the heart, a burning thrill,
Fired up by sheer strong will.

Peaks and valleys, paths unknown,
Travel we, but we're alone,
Forge ahead with eyes agleam,
Living out our wildest dream.

In the dusk, the light we chase,
Blaze of will, our saving grace,
In the end, we stand and shine,
Triumph of the will divine.

Kindle the Night

Stars ignite the darkened sky,
Dreams of old arise and fly,
Mystic whispers in the air,
Guiding spirits everywhere.

Candles lit with golden glow,
Secrets of the night bestow,
In the quiet, hearts unite,
Kindred souls in gentle light.

Through the twilight we embark,
Leaving trails that leave a mark,
Kindle the night, our spirits high,
Underneath the vast, bright sky.

Ecstasy of Pursuit

Rivers rush and mountains call,
In our quest, we give our all,
Chasing dreams that never end,
On this path, our hearts we lend.

Winds of fate, they guide our way,
Through the night and through the day,
With each step, our spirits bloom,
In the face of endless gloom.

Boundless sky and open sea,
In pursuit, we find we're free,
Ecstasy in every stride,
In this journey, we confide.

Chase the Horizon

Beneath the sky so vast and wide,
Where dreams and hopes so often hide,
We chase horizons far and near,
Guided by a distant star's soft cheer.

Mountains echo tales of old,
Rivers flow with secrets bold,
Step by step, we trek the dawn,
In pursuit of nights that are long gone.

Through meadows lush with morning dew,
Past twilight's glowing, vibrant hue,
We journey forth with hearts ablaze,
In the endless search of day's first rays.

The horizon calls with whispered song,
To a world where we belong,
Onward strides the traveler's heart,
Chasing dreams that never part.

Enthusiast's Chronicle

In pages worn and stories told,
Where dreams of yore were brave and bold,
An enthusiast's heart does leap and bound,
In every secret that is found.

With fervor bright and spirit keen,
They wander realms both seen and unseen,
Embracing life with open hand,
Seeking wonders across the land.

Each sunrise brings a brand new quest,
In riddles old they find their rest,
Their passion drives them ever fast,
To capture moments that will last.

From stars above to earth below,
Their chronicles in endless flow,
The world unfolds its rich delight,
In the enthusiast's zealous sight.

Heart Unbridled

In the quiet of a midnight's dream,
Where shadows play and moonbeams gleam,
A heart unbridled finds its way,
Through the labyrinth of night to day.

No chains can hold its wild desire,
Nor quench the ember of its fire,
It dances free on winds so high,
A melody beneath the sky.

With every beat, a story penned,
Of love and loss that has no end,
A saga wrought with joy and pain,
Yet never yielding to the rain.

In the pulses of the night,
It seeks the dawn, the coming light,
This heart unbridled, fierce and true,
Chasing dreams in skies of blue.

Lava of Yearning

Beneath the earth where fires rage,
Upon the heart's uncharted page,
Lava flows with yearning's heat,
In a symphony of ardent beat.

Passion burns in crimson tide,
Through veins where secrets often hide,
In whispers soft, it calls you near,
To feel the love both bold and clear.

Mountains tremble with desire,
As hearts forge in molten fire,
To shape a bond as strong as stone,
In places where the stars have shone.

The lava glows in endless dance,
A testament to each romance,
In the flames of yearning's rise,
Two souls unite 'neath burning skies.

Illuminate the Path

In shadows deep, the lantern glows,
A beacon bright where darkness sows.
Through winding roads and ancient stones,
It lights the way where courage roams.

Beyond the fear, beyond the doubt,
It whispers truths we can't live without.
A fire within that never fades,
Guiding us through life's endless shades.

When storms descend and skies obscure,
Its steady light remains so pure.
Through nights of sorrow, days of strife,
It carves the path that leads to life.

Unyielding Spirit

In the heart of battles fierce,
A spirit stands, unbent, not pierced.
Through tempests wild and trials grand,
It holds its ground with steadfast hand.

When shadows loom and voices tire,
It rises up, a burning fire.
No storm or wave can dim its flame,
An ageless force, forever named.

With every fall it finds its rise,
A strength unbound, beneath the skies.
In quiet moments, loud and clear,
It echoes on, defying fear.

Echoes of Fierceness

In the silence of the dawn,
A roar begins, though night has gone.
Across the valleys, to the seas,
It's carried far upon the breeze.

The echo of an iron will,
That bends no knee and takes no still.
Among the stars, beneath the earth,
It tells the tale of endless worth.

Through struggles vast, in wars we wage,
Its thunder speaks on every page.
A legacy of hearts so bold,
In echoes fierce, the story's told.

Vibrance of Dreams

In the quiet of the night,
A dream unfolds in colors bright.
A canvas wide, with stars to gleam,
It paints the world in vibrant dream.

Beyond the realm of doubt and fear,
A vision pure, a future clear.
Within its glow, the soul can see,
A boundless field of what can be.

Each ray of hope, each spark of light,
Merges to form a wondrous sight.
In dreams, we find the strength to soar,
To reach for all, and even more.

Chasing the Sun

Across the sky, beyond the sea,
We chase the sun eternally.
Its golden rays, they light our way,
From dawn to dusk, night to day.

Onward we stride with hearts so bold,
Seeking warmth in stories told.
By ancient fires, through whispers loud,
In unity, we rise and vow.

Shadows cast as daylight fades,
A legacy that never shades.
For even in the darkest night,
We find the strength to carry light.

Mountains tall and valleys wide,
We journey forth in steady stride.
Chasing the sun, our endless quest,
In every heart, we find our rest.

Heartbeats and Dreams

In the quiet of the night, hearts beat
To rhythms of dreams, soft and sweet.
Whispers of hope, caressing minds,
In dreams, the loose threads intertwine.

Through fields of gold and skies so blue,
We chase visions known only to a few.
With every heartbeat, a dream takes flight,
In silent embrace of the velvet night.

Eyes closed, yet worlds unfold,
A mosaic of stories, brave and bold.
Heartbeats sync in perfect time,
To the symphony of dreams, sublime.

By dawn's first light, dreams retreat,
To corners of minds, bittersweet.
But heartbeats hum a resolute tune,
To chase those dreams beneath the moon.

Fire in the Veins

With fire in the veins, we forge anew,
A path ignited by passions true.
Burning bright, we stand our ground,
In the dance of flames, we are found.

Every challenge, a spark we embrace,
Kindling our strength in life's fiery race.
Amidst the blaze, we find our core,
A spirit unyielding, wanting more.

Through ashes and smoke, hearts remain,
Beating strong with fiery refrain.
Embers glow in the darkest night,
Guiding us with their steadfast light.

Unbroken bonds, forged in the heat,
Every victory, every heartbeat.
Fire in the veins, we never tire,
Unquenchable flames, our eternal fire.

Soulful Journeys

On soulful journeys, we embark,
Navigating through light and dark.
With every step, we seek, we find,
Pieces of ourselves, intertwined.

The road is long, the path unknown,
Yet every mile, our spirit's grown.
With eyes wide open, hearts set free,
We chase what is and what could be.

Through storm and sun, we travel far,
Guided by dreams, our northern star.
Each soulful journey tells a tale,
Of hope and love, where fears grow pale.

In unity, we find our way,
Through night and dawn, to brightest day.
Soulful journeys, endless and grand,
Together we walk, hand in hand.

Compelled by Fire

In darkness shone a flicker bright,
A spark that danced in endless night.
It whispered tales of warmth unknown,
A pyre of dreams in hearts alone.

With fierce resolve, it grew and spread,
Its flames of hope in colors red.
It urged the timid to aspire,
Compelled by whispers of the fire.

In embers' glow the spirits soared,
Dispelled the shadows fears had stored.
The blaze unveiled the hidden path,
A guide through sorrow, pain, and wrath.

The Roar Inside

A tempest brews within the chest,
A roar that drowns in silent rest.
It yearns to break the chains that bind,
    Unleash the fury of the mind.

Through whispered winds and thunder's cry,
It seeks the truth where echoes lie.
A force unbridled, wild and vast,
A storm of soul, its shadows cast.

With every pulse, the roar persists,
Defies the dark, the chains it twists.
A battle fought on fields unseen,
The roar inside, forever keen.

Love's Inferno

In eyes that meet, a spark ignites,
A blaze that carves through moons and nights.
Two souls entwined in passion's glow,
An inferno where desires flow.

Through tempest winds and fateful dives,
Love's fire within them stays alive.
It burns with warmth, yet wild and free,
An endless dance, a symphony.

Their hearts a furnace, souls entwined,
In flames of love they are defined.
An ardent plea, a fervent call,
Love's inferno consumes them all.

Embers Turned Blaze

In the ashes, embers hid,
A silent hint of what once did.
Yet whispered sparks in twilight's haze,
Turn embers calm to frenzied blaze.

With breath of life, the fire renewed,
From past's embrace, the future brewed.
A phoenix from the dusk emerged,
In flames of hope, ambitions surged.

The blaze anew, in crimson light,
Cast shadows of the darkest night.
Through trials faced, the spirit raised,
From embers turned to brilliant blaze.

Ablaze with Dreams

Stars paint the sky, in silver streams,
Whispers of night, in quiet gleams.
Dreams take flight, on moonlit beams,
Hearts afire, with endless schemes.

In twilight's hold, our spirits roam,
Through valleys deep, to seas with foam.
Chasing shadows, where wild winds comb,
Ablaze with dreams, we find our home.

Mountains call, from peaks untold,
Forests thick, where secrets unfold.
Through the burning cold, and sunlit gold,
Dreamers wander, brave and bold.

Fired by Hope

In the darkest hour, when shadows creep,
Hope's gentle light begins to seep.
Through trials and paths so steep,
We find the strength to rise and leap.

Hearts of flame, with courage stoked,
Through tears and pain, unwavering hope.
With every doubt and fear we've broke,
The spirit ignites, finding its scope.

Through storm and calm, and night's embrace,
Hope's light endures, in every place.
Guiding us through time and space,
Our souls enlightened, by hope's grace.

Wild Hearts Ablaze

In fields of passion, we run free,
Wild hearts ablaze, 'neath ancient tree.
No chains or bonds constrain our plea,
For love and dreams, our wild decree.

Through tempest winds, and thunder's call,
We stand united, we will not fall.
Bearing the scars of life's great brawl,
Wild hearts, bright flames, standing tall.

With laughter loud, and spirits bold,
Our stories vibrant, yet to be told.
Through nights of silver, days of gold,
Wild hearts ablaze, a sight behold.

Path of Fierce Dreams

Walking the path of fierce dreams,
Rivers of passion in moonlit streams.
Through mountains high, and sunlight's beams,
Our spirits soar, unbound, it seems.

In valleys deep, where secrets lie,
We find our strength, beneath the sky.
Faces turned up, with a sigh,
Learning to dream, learning to fly.

With every step, through night and day,
Onward we march, come what may.
For in our hearts, there lies the way,
Path of fierce dreams, where hopes stay.

Fierce Pursuits

In the chase of dreams so bright,
Through the dark and through the night,
We ascend on wings of might,
To realms where stars ignite.

With hearts that never tire,
Fueled by an endless fire,
To heights we dare aspire,
Our spirits soaring higher.

The hardships we embrace,
With courage, not a trace,
Of fear within this place,
We run the ardent race.

In shadows we find light,
Our hopes are ever bright,
Each dawn a new insight,
In fierce pursuit of flight.

The journey never ends,
Around each bend, it sends,
New dreams to comprehend,
Our spirits shall transcend.

Heart's Wildfire

In the calm of morning dew,
Wakes a heart that's ever true,
With passions born anew,
And skies of endless blue.

Desires fiercely blaze,
Illuminating days,
In intricate displays,
Of love's enchanting maze.

With every whispered plea,
And every fleeting plea,
We set our spirits free,
In love's vast, stormy sea.

The fire burns so bright,
Guiding through the night,
A beacon pure and white,
Of hope within our sight.

Through trials and delight,
Our souls in fervent flight,
In heart's undying light,
We conquer every plight.

Embrace the Blaze

When life's a fiery storm,
In its fierce, untamed form,
We find amidst the swarm,
A place where hearts are warm.

To face the blazing tide,
Within our souls, we guide,
A strength we cannot hide,
With courage as our pride.

The heat that sears our way,
With every break of day,
Paves roads of golden clay,
For feet that will not stray.

Through tempests and through strife,
We celebrate this life,
With passion as a knife,
To carve through every rife.

In every burning glance,
In every daring dance,
We take our chance,
And in the blaze, advance.

Unquenchable Spirit

Beneath the starlit roof,
In times serene or aloof,
We find an inner truth,
In moments all too brief.

With spirits brave and bold,
Through days both hot and cold,
Our stories yet untold,
In hearts that we enfold.

Each obstacle, we greet,
With steadfast, steady feet,
Our hopes, they pulse and beat,
A symphony so sweet.

No force can douse our flame,
Or bring our hearts to shame,
For in our souls, the fame,
Of dreams we dare to claim.

The spirit that we bear,
Unyielding in despair,
Shows in the love we share,
With every breath, a prayer.

Unquenchable, we rise,
In life's eternal skies,
Our fire never dies,
A light for all to prize.

Pulse of Adventure

Where mountains meet the sky,
And rivers carve their path,
The wild calls with a sigh,
A dance of nature's wrath.

Within the forest deep,
Where shadows softly creep,
Dreams of wanderers sleep,
Their memories to keep.

From deserts vast and wide,
To oceans' endless tide,
The spirit seeks to glide,
With freedom as its guide.

Echoes of untamed lands,
And footprints in the sands,
The pulse of life expands,
Written by unseen hands.

Adventures yet unknown,
In whispers softly blown,
A journey all its own,
Where seeds of dreams are sown.

Sparks of Ambition

In the silence of the night,
Where dreams ignite the fight,
A spark begins to light,
Ambition takes its flight.

With courage as its friend,
And hopes that never bend,
The journey finds no end,
The will to break and mend.

Against the tides of doubt,
Where whispers scream and shout,
The heart maps out its route,
Ambition, strong and stout.

Upon the peak it stands,
With triumph in its hands,
And time obeys commands,
Laid out in careful plans.

With stars within its grasp,
And dreams it dares to clasp,
The future's in its ask,
Ambition wears its mask.

Passion's Promise

Beneath a moonlit sky,
Where echoes softly sigh,
A promise whispered by,
The depths of passion's cry.

In fields of endless blooms,
Bright petals pierce the gloom,
Lovers share the rooms,
Of hearts that learned to bloom.

With every tender glance,
In the dance of sweet romance,
The soul begins to prance,
In love's intoxicating trance.

Where words are not enough,
And edges become rough,
Passion seals with love,
The promise that's enough.

Forever side by side,
Through life's relentless tide,
With passion as their guide,
Together they will ride.

Electric Heartstrings

The rhythm of the night,
A pulse so pure and bright,
Through veins of endless light,
Electric heartstrings tight.

A symphony of dreams,
In neon-glow it streams,
Life's melody redeems,
Through vibrant, endless beams.

With every beat and tone,
The universe condones,
Connections overthrown,
In music's undertones.

From whispers to a roar,
Emotions to explore,
Electric, evermore,
A love to underscore.

Infinite and free,
In perfect harmony,
Heartstrings vibrate in glee,
A song of unity.

Fires That Guide

In the twilight's crimson glow,
Whispers of an ancient lore,
Through the shadows' silent flow,
Hearts ignite forevermore.

Kindling sparks of dreams unbound,
Lighting paths we dare not tread,
In the darkest night, profound,
Fires guide where angels bled.

With a flame that never wanes,
Hope and courage intertwined,
Through the tempest and the rains,
Guided by a force divine.

Silent echoes fill the night,
Bravery in embers bright,
Arrows drawn in fearless flight,
Phoenix rises, pure and white.

Faith and valor, hand in hand,
Fuel the fire's gentle blaze,
In the heart of every land,
Burns the light of endless days.

Zeal's Journey

Beyond the horizon's sweep,
Through valleys deep and wide,
Zeal's journey, shadows keep,
Guided by the stars inside.

Whispers of a boundless dream,
In each step, a silent plea,
Rivers cross and mountains gleam,
Zeal unchained, forever free.

Gales and tempests pave the way,
Every storm, a test to bear,
In the night and break of day,
Zeal's spirit, fierce and rare.

Paths entwined in destiny,
Echoes of a whispered quest,
Seek the skies eternally,
Zeal's heart beats within the chest.

Endless skies and oceans deep,
Dreams alight on wings of fire,
Through the stars, a journey's leap,
Zeal's desire, hearts' aspire.

Chronicles of Zeal

In the annals of our time,
Tales of valor, whispered low,
Chronicles in prose and rhyme,
Legends of a fervent glow.

Through the mire and through the mist,
Zeal's relentless, fervent stride,
Armored hearts and iron fists,
Facing dusk with currents tied.

Songs of heroes, songs of strife,
Etched in time, forever told,
Zeal's relentless grip on life,
Burns in hearts both young and old.

Every verse a battle cry,
Every word a lifeline cast,
In the chronicles, they lie,
Zeal's undying flame amassed.

To the future, tales bequeath,
Whispers of a time so grand,
Chronicles in every breath,
Zeal's journey, hand in hand.

Pyre of Dreams

In the hearth of night, they bloom,
Dreams alight in sacred fire,
Flames that chase away the gloom,
Cinders of the heart's desire.

Each a blaze of pure intent,
Woven light in realms unseen,
On the pyre, dreams are sent,
Burning bright, serene and keen.

Phoenix wings of hope arise,
From the ashes, spirits soar,
Dreams awaken in the skies,
Burning evermore, encore.

Through the darkest nights they shine,
Dreams aflame in endless light,
Every ember so divine,
Guiding through the endless night.

Sacred fire, pure and bright,
In the pyre, dreams ignite,
In their glow, the future's sight,
Woven in the softest night.

Flames of Tomorrow

In the ashes of today,
New hopes take flight.
Whispers of dawn,
Through the dark night.

Amber sparks ignite,
Future's grand light.
Building dreams anew,
From embers so bright.

Winds of change swirl,
Through realms unseen.
Crafting destinies grand,
In a world serene.

Under twilight's veil,
Stars softly gleam.
Guiding hearts forward,
In a rhapsodic dream.

Flames of tomorrow,
Dance in the sky.
Promising a radiant,
New horizon nigh.

Echoes of Fire

In the realm of twilight,
Where shadows play,
An ancient flame echoes,
Through night and day.

Crimson tongues whisper,
Legends untold.
Flickers of wisdom,
In embers of old.

Sparks fly high,
Reach for the stars.
Illuminating paths,
Leaving no scars.

Hearts ablaze,
With fierce desire.
Dreams resurrected,
By echoes of fire.

In the silent night,
A whisper grows.
Through time it lingers,
And forever flows.

Luster of Dreams

In the silent night,
Dreams take their flight.
Glittering like stars,
In the moon's soft light.

Soft whispers carry,
Wishes so grand.
In the realm of dreams,
We take our stand.

Visions unfold,
In a radiant gleam.
Hearts beat in tune,
With the luster of dreams.

Futures foreseen,
In silken threads.
Hope intertwines,
With golden spreads.

Awake with dawn,
Dreams linger still.
Guiding us gently,
With an endless thrill.

Burning Quest

In hearts of fire,
A quest begins.
Driven by dreams,
From deep within.

Through trials and storms,
We forge our way.
Guided by passion,
Night and day.

Bound by our fate,
Yet free to choose.
With each step forward,
We refuse to lose.

Mountains we climb,
Valleys so deep.
In pursuit of dreams,
Wide awake, not asleep.

The burning quest,
Leads us anew.
To paths uncharted,
With skies so blue.

Intense Horizons

The sky ablaze with fiery hues,
A canvas painted deep with blues,
Horizons stretching far and wide,
A world where mysteries reside.

Winds that whisper tales untold,
Mountains standing strong and bold,
Each step forward, past renews,
The dawn reflects in morning's dews.

Rivers carve their timeless song,
Through valleys where the spirits throng,
A journey where the heart expands,
Horizons shaped by nature's hands.

Stars ignite the evening sky,
Guiding dreams that soar up high,
An endless reach, no bounds defined,
Intense horizons, deeply twined.

Hearts awake to morning's cast,
Chasing shadows, moving fast,
In every sunrise, there's a sign,
New worlds on horizons shine.

Passionate Whispers

In the silence of the night,
Passionate whispers take their flight,
Softly stirring hearts anew,
Echoes of a love so true.

Moonlight dances on the floor,
Inviting dreams to soar and more,
Every secret, every glance,
Lives a timeless, daring chance.

Leaves that rustle in the breeze,
Conversations with the trees,
Nature's heartbeat, soft and low,
Nurturing the seeds we sow.

Eyes that meet and hearts that race,
Every touch, a warm embrace,
In the quiet, love confides,
Whispers travel far and wide.

Echoes fading like the mist,
Every word a fleeting kiss,
In the stillness, flames ignite,
Passionate whispers, pure delight.

The Fire Keeper

In the heart of ancient nights,
The fire keeper guards the lights,
Flames that flicker, dance and sway,
Through the shadows, guide the way.

Hands that tend the glowing blaze,
Sparkling embers, warming haze,
Stories shared from far and near,
In the fire, truths appear.

Eyes that watch with wisdom old,
Guard the secrets, tales untold,
Through the dark, the fire's might,
Keeps the cold of night in flight.

Voices whisper, crackling sound,
Around the fire, souls are found,
In the glow, connections deep,
Through the keeper's watch, they keep.

Morning comes with softest hues,
Fire dimmed, the night reviews,
The keeper's vigil, through the night,
Leaves a legacy of light.

Journey with Sparks

On paths where dreams and stardust blend,
A journey starts, no known end,
With every step, a spark we chase,
A quest through time and boundless space.

Feet that wander, hearts that roam,
Finding solace far from home,
Every crossroad, choice ignites,
Adventures born in starry nights.

Whispers of the past confined,
In sparks, our future well-defined,
Moving forward, casting fears,
On this road, through all the years.

Mountains call with peaks so high,
Valleys where the echoes lie,
In the spark of every turn,
Lessons of the heart we learn.

Hands that reach and souls that find,
Bound by threads of dream aligned,
In the journey, sparks do bind,
Eternal dance of heart and mind.

Burning Voyage

Upon the waves of molten dreams,
We sail through fire's endless streams,
A vessel forged in heat's embrace,
Seeks horizons far from place.

Flames that dance upon the bow,
Guide us through the inferno's vow,
Heat and light, our steady crew,
Toward the dawn, our spirits flew.

Ashen winds and ember skies,
Mirror hearts that never die,
Journey through the burning night,
With a soul that's pure and bright.

Tides of fire and seas ablaze,
Through horizon's molten glaze,
Seeks a land of cool and calm,
Yet cherishes this fiery balm.

In this voyage of flame and zeal,
Every spark and blaze we feel,
Becomes a tale we proudly tell,
Of a voyage through the fire's hell.

Scorched Horizons

Beyond the fields where shadows rest,
Lies a world by flames caressed,
The horizon's edge, a scarlet line,
Marks the start of trials divine.

Blistering winds across the plains,
Whisper secrets through the flames,
Every ember's gentle sigh,
Speaks of lands where phoenix fly.

Mountains rise in ashen peaks,
Where the earth in fury speaks,
Scorched horizons far and wide,
Hold the promise, hearts abide.

Stars that burn with fierce delight,
Guide us through the endless night,
Onward to the molten crest,
Where our hopes and dreams are blessed.

In the blaze of twilight's glow,
Where the fire's rivers flow,
Scorched horizons light the way,
To a dawn of a new day.

Flame-Touched Wings

A phoenix rises from the dark,
With flame-touched wings, it leaves a mark,
Across the sky in arcs of gold,
Its story, in the heat, is told.

Feathers bright with fire's kiss,
In the dawn, it finds its bliss,
Soaring high above the earth,
A testament to its rebirth.

Through the smoke and through the fire,
With a heart that beats with tire,
Returns again from ash and flame,
Never bound to stay the same.

In the dance of wings alight,
Carving through the endless night,
A phoenix teaches us to trust,
In the cycle—rise from dust.

With flame-touched wings, to skies it clings,
Spreading hope as it sings,
A song of fiery rebirth,
A promise of eternal worth.

Burning with Resolve

In the heart where passions lie,
Burns a flame that will not die,
Strength that rises with the dawn,
Echoes long when we are gone.

With resolve as fierce as fire,
We ascend, our spirits higher,
Every challenge, every strife,
Shapes the forge that forms our life.

Eyes that face the blazing heat,
Hands that do not know defeat,
In the trials that we embrace,
Find the courage, find the grace.

Through the furnace of the soul,
We emerge as something whole,
Burning with a pure intent,
To give the world our testament.

In the steady, glowing light,
Of resolve that burns so bright,
We become a living flame,
Writing history with our name.

Enthusiast's Odyssey

Beyond the hills where dreams reside,
A path untrodden calls our stride.
With every step, horizons new,
Adventure swirls in skies of blue.

Through forests dense and rivers wide,
We chase the secrets world would hide.
With hearts alight, and spirits bold,
We weave our tales, forever told.

In twilight's glow or morning's light,
Our journey thrusts us into flight.
A quest for meaning, joy and pride,
In life's grand odyssey we bide.

The constellations guide our way,
Through nights of wonder, skies of gray.
With laughter's echo, tears that cleanse,
We write a saga that transcends.

When final steps meet sunset's hue,
We'll know our passions forged us true.
Enthusiasts, forever free,
In odyssey, eternally.

A Blaze Within

A spark ignites within the core,
A flame that burns forevermore.
With passion's heat, our souls we mold,
A fire in hearts, both young and old.

Through trials harsh and winds that blow,
The blaze within will fiercely glow.
Our dreams, the fuel that we confide,
In flames of courage, we abide.

In shadows dark and valleys deep,
The embers of our spirit keep.
A light that guides, a warming breath,
Defying fear, embracing death.

With every challenge, scorch and sear,
Our inner fire remains sincere.
It drives us forth, through storm and rain,
A testament to hope and gain.

In twilight's dusk or dawn's new flame,
Our blaze within shall stake its claim.
A beacon bright, in hearts we trust,
With every ember, rise we must.

Ember and Flame

In whispers soft, the embers speak,
Of hidden fires, passions deep.
Their glow a promise, fierce and grand,
A tale of flame, by fate's command.

The ember's warmth, it gently grows,
A potent force the spirit knows.
From timid spark to roaring bright,
Flame burgeons forth, a brilliant sight.

Through nights of cold, and days so bleak,
Embers persist, our strength they seek.
With steady rise, and fiery art,
The flame ignites within the heart.

Together joined, ember and flame,
They forge a bond, they stake a claim.
In unity, a blaze is born,
To light the way, till break of morn.

In every soul, this pair resides,
A force that burns and never hides.
Ember and flame, a dance so wild,
Within our spirits, fierce and mild.

Unstoppable Force

Through walls of steel and barriers high,
With relentless will, we touch the sky.
An unstoppable force, we rise anew,
With every challenge, breaking through.

With hearts of courage, minds so keen,
We pierce the veil, unseen, serene.
Our strength, a tidal wave of grace,
No obstacle can hold its place.

In every storm, through darkest night,
Our force propels us into flight.
Unyielding spirit, boundless drive,
In every beat, we feel alive.

No chains can bind, no shackles hold,
Our destiny, in hands so bold.
An endless surge, a rhythmic course,
We are the world's unstoppable force.

With every stride, with every leap,
In dreams and deeds, our spirit's steep.
An unstoppable force, we claim,
A legacy in timeless name.

Unstoppable Zeal

In the hush of dawn's bright hue,
Dreams untouched begin to brew.
With a heart that's bold and true,
We chase skies, both clear and blue.

Mountains tall and rivers vast,
Paths untrodden in the past.
Through the winds we journey fast,
Making moments forever last.

Eyes aglow with passion's fire,
Climbing ever, rising higher.
Boundless dreams our only sire,
Hearts resound with sacred choir.

Fields of gold and endless green,
Mine the wonders yet unseen.
In our spirit so serene,
Lives the quest, the evergreen.

With a will that won't abate,
Stride by stride, we carve our fate.
Facing challenges so great,
We, the ones who dominate.

Inferno of Hopes

Flames that dance within our soul,
Hopes ignite and take their toll.
In the heart of every goal,
Burning bright, we find our role.

Stars align in fiery trails,
Guiding us through stormy gales.
In the night where silence wails,
Hope's inferno never fails.

Every spark and ember's gleam,
Paints the picture of our dream.
In the river of time's stream,
Hopes unite in one great theme.

In the ashes of despair,
Rise the dreams beyond compare.
Carving pathways in the air,
Filling hearts that dare to care.

Fiery visions pure and grand,
Crafting futures hand in hand.
In the blaze we'll firmly stand,
Hopes inferno sweeps the land.

Song of the Zealot

With a fervent voice we raise,
Melodies of zeal and praise.
Through the nights and endless days,
Singing loud in golden rays.

Passion's chords within our chest,
Strike a tune that won't attest.
Living life by no behest,
In our zeal, we're truly blessed.

Every heartbeat's rhythmic sound,
Echoes through the world around.
In our cause, we're ever bound,
Standing firm on holy ground.

Sweeping winds that carry light,
Through the storm and darkest night.
In our song, there is no fright,
Just the shine of pure delight.

With a fervor strong and pure,
We are bound to hearts ensure.
In our zeal, we find the cure,
For a life that's bright, demure.

Glowing with Potential

In the seed of every thought,
Lies a world yet to be sought.
In the dreams that we've been taught,
Glows the future we have wrought.

Every challenge, every test,
Forms the journey of our quest.
In the striving to be best,
Potential glows within our chest.

Stars above and earth below,
Witness to the seeds we sow.
In our minds the visions grow,
With the light we fiercely show.

Through the shadows, through the rain,
In our hearts we feel no pain.
Glowing bright, we break the chain,
In the end, we shall attain.

From the spark that moves us on,
To the break of each new dawn.
In our souls, the fire's drawn,
Potential glowing, never gone.

Dancing on the Edge

Twilight's whispers guide our way,
As moonlight bends and shadows play,
To the rhythm of night, we sway,
Dancing on the edge of day.

Stars above in silent cheer,
Steps entwined through dreams, so near,
Bound by moments, pure and clear,
Dancing on the edge of fear.

Velvet skies in twilight's embrace,
Trace the contours of your face,
Caught in time, a fleeting grace,
Dancing on the edge of space.

In each twirl, horizons blend,
Infinite, where the heart can mend,
To the night's soft call, we bend,
Dancing on the edge, my friend.

By dawn's light, a new page turns,
Fading stars, yet our spirit burns,
In our hearts, the dance returns,
Dancing on the edge, love yearns.

Whispers of Euphoria

In the silence, echoes rise,
Softest murmurs, gentle sighs,
Euphoria's whispers in disguise,
Bringing light to shaded skies.

Through the maze of thought, we steer,
Chasing dreams both bright and clear,
In each whisper, love austere,
Binds us close, and draws us near.

Moments fleeting, yet so grand,
Euphoria takes our hand,
Guiding through an unknown land,
Gardens grow from whispered strand.

Lost in time, yet ever found,
Whispers form a joy profound,
In their song, we're tightly bound,
Hearts that soar with every sound.

In each breath, a story told,
Whispers weave a thread of gold,
Euphoria's embrace, so bold,
In its warmth, our dreams unfold.

Blaze of Aspirations

In the forge of dreams we cast,
Visions bold, from futures past,
Through the sky, hopes flying fast,
In a blaze of aspirations, vast.

Fires ignite in every heart,
Crafting tales with passion's art,
Dreams and goals, not far apart,
In the blaze, we each take part.

Mountains tall, we aim to scale,
With the wind, our fervent sail,
Through each storm and gentle gale,
Blaze of aspirations prevails.

In our eyes, a spark divine,
Guided by an unseen sign,
Pathways lit by stars align,
Blaze of aspirations, shine.

When shadows darken, we hold tight,
Through the night and toward the light,
In hopes' blaze, we find our flight,
Aspirations guiding right.

Heart's Crusade

In the dawn of love's first light,
Heart embarks on noble fight,
Through the valleys, day and night,
On a crusade, pure and bright.

Battles fought with silent tears,
Overcome the deepest fears,
In each pulse, the path appears,
Heart's crusade through wear and years.

Oceans cross and mountains climb,
Songs of love in perfect rhyme,
In each heartbeat's endless chime,
Heart's crusade defies all time.

Guided by a truth so deep,
Promises we vow to keep,
In our souls, the embers leap,
Heart's crusade in love, we steep.

At journey's end, yet still we dare,
In the light, our souls lay bare,
With each beat, a silent prayer,
Heart's crusade, forever there.

Inexhaustible Thunder

Thunder rumbles through the night,
Chasing shadows in their flight,
Endless echoes, bold and vast,
Moments etched, forever cast.

Clouds convene in darkened shape,
Nature's force, it can't escape,
Rivers flood and winds do scream,
Rending silence, break the seam.

Mountains tremble, valleys quake,
In the storm's wake, we awake,
Electric touch on skin so bare,
In the chaos, beauty's lair.

Eyes wide open to the storm,
Heartbeats racing, pulses warm,
Life's ferocity, bold and grand,
In thunder's grip, we understand.

Distant skies may settle soon,
Still the thunder sings its tune,
In its roar, we find our might,
Inexhaustible, pure, and bright.

A Journey Aflame

Blazing trails through dusk and dawn,
Footsteps marking paths long gone,
Fire's whisper, guiding light,
Through the shadows, dark of night.

Woods and fields, the flame does trace,
Leaving embers, their embrace,
Journeys taken, hearts set free,
In the spark of destiny.

Rivers wild and mountains bold,
Stories of the brave retold,
Each step forward, fervor's glow,
Where the daring dare to go.

Courage kindles in the soul,
Every ember, burning coal,
Dreams ignited, spirits fly,
Underneath a blazing sky.

When the flames at last subside,
And the heart's wild rhythm's tried,
Echoes of the fiery quest,
Linger on, forever blessed.

Roaring into Life

From the stillness, comes a roar,
Life's bold entrance at the door,
Breath of fire, soul's resound,
In this moment, hearts unbound.

Echoes through the verdant plains,
Streaming light through windowpanes,
Every beat of heart and drum,
Roaring life, here we come.

Oceans wide and skies alight,
Daybreak dancing into night,
Every ripple, every wave,
Roaring life, the brave and brave.

Mountains call with ancient voice,
Hearken, make a daring choice,
Leap and bound, the world invite,
Roaring into life's delight.

Endless journeys, paths anew,
Life's great canvas, never blue,
Roar and whisper, triumph song,
Roaring life, forever strong.

Radiance Unfazed

Through the mist, a light unfazed,
Soft and steady, evening razed,
Glow that dances 'cross the tide,
Radiance, it won't subside.

Stars ignite the velvet night,
Guiding sailors to the light,
Beacon bold, a steady gaze,
In the dark, its warmth amaze.

Morning sun, atop the hill,
Gentle rays that never still,
Touch the hearts, the souls of few,
With a light, both pure and true.

Candles flicker in the breeze,
Lighting pathways with such ease,
Radiance in every spark,
Guiding through, when days are dark.

Through all times, both bright and gray,
Radiance finds its gentle way,
In the hearts of those who see,
Light unfazed, eternally.

Hearts Enthralled

In twilight's gentle, tender embrace,
Two souls entwined, find their own grace.
Whispers of affection softly fall,
A symphony of hearts enthralled.

Under moon's serene, mystic light,
Love blooms in the quiet of night.
Eyes speak where words dare hesitate,
Destiny draws two hearts in fate.

Hands interlaced, promise exchanged,
In realms unknown, love unchained.
Infinite stars witness the bind,
Of two hearts, in twilight's find.

Dreams converge on paths unknown,
No longer shall they walk alone.
With every beat, a story told,
Of hearts enthralled, both brave and bold.

In love's canvas brightly restored,
True beauty in silence underscored.
Every glance and every sound,
In endless love, two souls found.

Passionate Embers

In the quiet of night, flames ignite,
Burning whispers of pure delight.
Heat rises, in fervent dance,
Embers glow in love's trance.

Crimson skies herald fate,
Two souls drawn to passion's gate.
Every touch, a spark anew,
Love's eternal fire, bold and true.

Beneath the stars, in shadows' play,
Desires weave, in bold array.
Hands explore, in tender quest,
Heartbeats quicken, two lovers blessed.

Flames entwined, in fervor's blaze,
In love's pyre, they find their ways.
Passionate embers, in soft gleam,
Burning bright in midnight's dream.

With every sigh, with every breath,
Life renews, in passion's depth.
Timeless dance of fire and soul,
Passionate embers, hearts made whole.

Rise of the Phoenix

From ashes deep, a spark ignites,
A tale of courage, silent nights.
Wings of flame, to skies ascend,
A soul reborn, with strength to lend.

In trials' forge, it found its way,
Through darkened paths, to light of day.
Fire within, fierce and bright,
A phoenix soars, in boundless flight.

Scars of past, in flame undone,
Emerge anew, beneath the sun.
Hope rekindled, soaring high,
A story penned in endless sky.

Charred remains, of sorrow's bind,
Transformed in heat, of will and mind.
Rise, oh phoenix, in glory's hue,
Embrace the dawn, a life anew.

In life's turmoil, strength is found,
In flames of hope, forever bound.
Rise of the phoenix, bold and free,
An endless testament to eternity.

Captive Fire

Behind the veil, the shadows dance,
A flicker of light, a stolen glance.
In depths unknown, a fire breathes,
Captive soul, in silent wreaths.

Chains of doubt, in twilight's shroud,
Love's ember waits, beneath the cloud.
Hearts confined, yet burn so bright,
In secret chambers, out of sight.

Whispered dreams, in silent night,
Passion's fire, in boundless flight.
Hidden realms, where hearts aspire,
To break free, from captive fire.

Unseen flames, in shadows' play,
Yearn the dawn, to kiss the day.
In darkness born, yet fiercely yearn,
For liberty, where passions burn.

Through tear's veil, and hopeful sigh,
Fire seeks, the open sky.
Captive hearts, in love's desire,
Break the chains and rise in fire.

Rapture and Flame

In whispers of dawn, our dreams take flight,
Through misty veils, in the quiet night.
Tender breaths, our hearts ignite,
Rapture and flame, in love's pure light.

Boundless skies where our spirits soar,
Beyond the shores of time's old lore.
In unity, our souls implore,
Rapture and flame, forevermore.

Silent echoes in the vast expanse,
Eternal dance, in a timeless trance.
Impassioned gaze, a single glance,
Rapture and flame in sweet romance.

Glistening stars in the velvet haze,
Lovers' vow in the endless maze.
Radiant hearts that forever blaze,
Rapture and flame in endless praise.

In every kiss, a promise kept,
In tranquil peace, where dreams are wept.
Through life's unknowns, our bond is prepped,
Rapture and flame where souls have leapt.

Sparks of Triumph

In shadows deep, where doubts reside,
We kindle flames, where fears abide.
With steely resolve and hearts untied,
Sparks of triumph, our spirits guide.

Through stormy nights and endless plight,
Our courage gleams, a beacon's light.
In unity, we stand upright,
Sparks of triumph in darkest night.

In fields of struggle, where dreams collide,
Resilient hope, our trusted guide.
Unwavering faith through peril's tide,
Sparks of triumph, we cannot hide.

With every step, a challenge faced,
Through trials stern, where dreams are chased.
Triumphant hearts leave no trace,
Sparks of triumph in victory's grace.

From ashes cold, where defeat lay,
We rise anew, with dawn of day.
In every heart, a will to stay,
Sparks of triumph light the way.

Desire's Flames

In twilight hues where shadows play,
Our hearts converge, we find our way.
Joined by fate, no words to say,
Desire's flames, ignite the day.

In stolen glances, secrets told,
A passion fierce, a love so bold.
In tender moments, pure gold,
Desire's flames, our souls behold.

Through silken nights and whispered sighs,
Our spirits dance beneath the skies.
In every touch, a new sunrise,
Desire's flames in lovers' eyes.

In every heartbeat, love's refrain,
A blazing fire through joy and pain.
Together bound in love's domain,
Desire's flames will ever reign.

As seasons change and time unfolds,
Our love, a story to be told.
In every breath, a feeling old,
Desire's flames, forever bold.

Vigorous Hearts

In the pulse of life, where strength is shown,
With every beat, our courage grown.
In unity, we're not alone,
Vigorous hearts in strength have flown.

Through trials faced and battles won,
With every rise, a brighter sun.
In concert, we are all as one,
Vigorous hearts, the race begun.

In silent prayers and shouted cries,
Our spirits lift to meet the skies.
Through teardrops shed and joyful eyes,
Vigorous hearts, where hope applies.

In fields of green and valleys wide,
Our dreams take root and there abide.
With steadfast love, as constant guide,
Vigorous hearts, in love confide.

In every dawn, where light breaks free,
Our boundless quest for destiny.
Together strong, with hearts' decree,
Vigorous hearts, eternally.

Undying Drive

Through shadows deep, we carve our way,
Unyielding hearts by night and day,
With strength unknown, we rise and strive,
In every breath, our dreams survive.

The dawn may break with endless trials,
Yet hope remains in silent miles,
Our spirit's flame will never cease,
In steadfast steps, we find our peace.

Mountains high and valleys low,
With tireless might, our passions grow,
No storm or drought can quell our fire,
For undying drive is our desire.

We stand as one, a force so strong,
With every challenge, we belong,
In unity, our purpose thrives,
Together bound, our dreams arrive.

Through endless night and magic skies,
Our souls ascend, we touch the prize,
For every fall, we rise anew,
In undying drive, our dreams come true.

Fevered Dreams

In night's embrace, our visions soar,
Through fevered dreams, we seek for more,
A world unknown, where shadows play,
In mystic realms, by moonlit sway.

The stars ignite with whispered tales,
Of limitless realms and timeless sails,
Through silver streams, our spirits dance,
In fevered dreams, we take a chance.

Each breath we hold, a glimpse we see,
Of what could be, of those who'll be,
A symphony of hopes and fears,
In fevered dreams, time disappears.

Through twilight hues and phantom light,
We chase the dawn, embrace the night,
In shadows deep, our spirits gleam,
For all is real in fevered dream.

With dawn's arrival, dreams may fade,
But in our hearts, their mark is made,
For in the night, our visions sing,
Through fevered dreams, our souls take wing.

Unleashed Aspirations

From chains we break, our spirits rise,
Unleashed, we claim the endless skies,
With fervent heart and boundless soul,
In every stride, we make us whole.

The world is vast, with dreams untamed,
Our spirits wild, by none are framed,
Through valleys deep and peaks unknown,
Unleashed, our aspirations grown.

With courage firm, we face the fate,
No fear can halt nor doubts berate,
In freedom's grasp, we soar so high,
Unleashed, we touch the bluest sky.

For in our hearts, a fire does burn,
To seek, to find, to always yearn,
With every breath, our spirits sing,
Unleashed, our aspirations spring.

Together bound, we chart the seas,
With faith and strength, through every breeze,
In unity, our dreams ignite,
Unleashed, we shine through darkest night.

Fiery Pathways

Through flames of time, we carve our way,
On fiery paths, by night and day,
With burning hearts, our spirits soar,
In every step, we seek for more.

Amidst the blaze, our courage gleams,
Through fiery pathways, fueled by dreams,
In forge of trials, we find our might,
Emboldened flames, our guiding light.

The shadows cast by dawn's embrace,
In fiery paths, we find our place,
With every spark, our hopes ignite,
Through searing trails, we rise in light.

No storm can quench our inner fire,
With every breath, we climb up higher,
On paths of flame, we tread with grace,
In every stride, a new embrace.

Together, through the fire, we stand,
In unity, we brave the land,
For in our hearts, the embers glow,
Through fiery pathways, dreams bestow.

Alight with Vision

In twilight's gentle embrace,
Where dreams begin to trace,
A future not yet seen,
Alights with vision's gleam.

Through shadows cold and deep,
Where whispers softly creep,
A hope begins to rise,
In ever-brilliant skies.

With courage, hearts ignite,
In passion's fervent light,
Each step a bold delight,
Through day and darkest night.

In every fleeting thought,
A universe is wrought,
Alight with endless scheme,
In the visionary dream.

So cast your gaze afar,
Hold tight to every star,
For what will come, will be,
A world by vision free.

Dreamer's Bonfire

Amid the night's embrace,
Where silent stars efface,
A dreamer's heart takes flight,
In bonfire's gentle light.

In gleaming ember's glow,
The unseen paths do grow,
A whisper in the breeze,
That dances through the trees.

Beneath the sky so vast,
Where moments seem to last,
A flicker in the dark,
Ignites the fervent spark.

With every breath, aspire,
In dreamer's bold desire,
To reach beyond the veil,
Where endless dreams prevail.

The flames of hope ascend,
Where wish and wonder blend,
In bonfire's warming hue,
The dreamer's soul anew.

Inferno of Zeal

With heartbeats racing fast,
In fervor's mighty blast,
A blaze of passion's seal,
The inferno of zeal.

Through trials fierce and strong,
Where echoes of belong,
A will that never yields,
In unrelenting fields.

The winds of change may howl,
Yet in the fire a vow,
To stand and face the storm,
In zeal's undying form.

In every challenge, rise,
With fire within the eyes,
A force of boundless might,
In zeal's relentless light.

Embrace each burning flame,
With fearless, brilliant aim,
For in the zeal's bright core,
A spirit will explore.

Quest for Radiance

Upon the dawn's first ray,
Where shadows fade away,
A quest for radiance true,
Begins with morning's hue.

Through valleys wide and far,
Beneath the twinkling star,
A journey intertwined,
With light that leads the blind.

In every step, a spark,
To guide through night so dark,
In search of golden beams,
Beyond the realm of dreams.

The path may twist and bend,
But light will never end,
For in the heart's bright gleam,
Resides the radiant beam.

So onward, venture bold,
With stories yet untold,
In quest for radiance pure,
A light that will endure.

Radiant Desires

In the quiet dawn light's embrace,
We chase the dreams we dare to face,
Shadows yield to morning's glow,
In this warmth, our hopes bestow.

Beneath the skies, so wide and free,
Our fleeting breaths a symphony,
Whispers of a world akin,
To the boundless fire within.

Stars align above our stride,
Guiding us with gleaming pride,
Through the night, where fears reside,
In love's radiance, we confide.

Hearts ignite in brilliant beams,
Sailing through the realm of dreams,
Echoes in the silent night,
Calling forth the soul's delight.

Together in this journey vast,
Hand in hand, we shall outlast,
Every trial, every fight,
Radiant desires in our sight.

Path of Flames

Upon the path where embers gleam,
We walk amidst the dreamer's stream,
With every step, a fiery tale,
In passion's blaze, we will prevail.

Through forests dense, where shadows creep,
In shadows' murk, our secrets keep,
Guardians of an ancient pyre,
To live, to love, through heart's desire.

The winds of fate shall fan the spark,
Guiding us through dark and stark,
In the flame, our courage wakes,
Lighting paths where fear abates.

In every tear and joyous laugh,
We find the strength, we chart the path,
Through the trials and through the pain,
Flames of hope, we shall sustain.

With every dawn, we rise anew,
In fire's glow, our spirits drew,
A path of flames, a journey bright,
Through the darkness, into light.

Limitless Passion

Beneath the stars, where dreams take flight,
We soar through realms of endless night,
In hearts ablaze, where passions burn,
To the cosmos, our souls return.

Through realms of time, where legends flow,
We traverse paths where lovers go,
Bound by threads of fate's design,
In this dance, our spirits shine.

From whispers soft to roars on high,
We transcend space, we touch the sky,
In every glance, a world anew,
Boundless love in every view.

In moments where the worlds align,
We find the truth in each divine,
Harmony of souls entwined,
In limitless passion, intertwined.

Beyond the veil of earthly ties,
We reach for stars in endless skies,
Together in this boundless flight,
Infinite hearts, in endless light.

Ember of Hope

In the quiet of the night's retreat,
An ember glows, a heartbeat neat,
Where shadows dance, in silent cope,
We find within, the ember of hope.

Through storms that rage and winds that wail,
We guard the spark that will not fail,
In every trial, every slope,
We cling to faith, an ember of hope.

With every dawn's renewing grace,
We find the strength, to face the chase,
Through valleys deep and mountains steep,
The ember's glow, our hearts will keep.

In dreams foretold by whispered lore,
We fight, we love, and then explore,
Through darkest nights, our spirits cope,
Guided by that ember of hope.

Together in the twilight glow,
We nurture flames that softly grow,
In every heart and every soul,
An ember of hope makes us whole.

Fierce Determination

The mountains loom, so cold and high,
But I shall reach towards the sky,
With every step, each labored breath,
I banish fear, the thought of death.

Across the valleys, through the night,
I push and strive, pursue the light,
For in my heart, where dreams reside,
It's there, with strength, I'll find my stride.

No storm or tempest's wrath shall break,
The iron will which I now take,
For through the dark, my path is clear,
With fierce resolve, I'll conquer fear.

In trials faced, my spirit soars,
Each challenge met unlocks new doors,
With grit and might, I'll claim my fate,
Persistent heart, resilient state.

So let the world throw what it may,
With fierce determination, I won't sway,
To heights unknown, my spirit flies,
For in my heart, my courage lies.

Enthralled Persistency

In shadows deep where fears reside,
A brighter fire will soon collide,
With hands unyielding, holding tight,
I chase the dawn, dispel the night.

No path too rough, no journey long,
With strength within, I'm ever strong,
Through trials harsh, and pain endured,
My spirit's flame remains assured.

Lost dreams revive, where hopes align,
In hallowed halls of heart and mind,
With every step, persistence grows,
In this resolve, my spirit shows.

A beacon shines, though clouds may loom,
Persistent light in darkened room,
For in each walk, each stride I take,
My will unbroken, none shall shake.

Through every storm, through every strife,
With seasoned heart, I carve my life,
Enthralled by dreams, forever bent,
On paths that lead to firmament.

So forward march, with vision clear,
Enthralled persistency draws near,
The journey's end, a place of grace,
With steadfast heart, I've won the race.

Committed to the Fire

In the forge where dreams are made,
Stand firm, resolved, without dismay,
With molten heart and purpose dire,
I brave the storm, commit to fire.

Through embers bright, a path I tread,
With courage pure and strength unsaid,
Each trial burns, refines my soul,
In flames of life, I find my goal.

Through ash and smoke, I still ascend,
For dreams will not break, nor will they bend,
With every spark, my spirit burns,
To reach for more, my heart it yearns.

No tempests fierce, nor torrid flame,
Can dim my light, nor quench my aim,
For in the blaze, a truth is told,
In fire's heart, my dreams unfold.

With passion deep, and purpose clear,
To destinies, I now draw near,
Committed thus to fire's embrace,
In burning light, I find my place.

Spirit Ablaze

In twilight's glow, my spirit wakes,
To dreams ignited, no mistake,
With soul on fire, ablaze with might,
I journey forth into the night.

In shadows cast, the path unknown,
I tread with faith, my strength has grown,
For in the flame, the truth I see,
My spirit's call to destiny.

A blaze of hope, a torch I bear,
Through trials, fears, and whispered dare,
With undimmed eyes, I chase the day,
My heart alight, I find my way.

Through valleys deep, where shadows lie,
My spirit climbs, a burning sky,
For in each spark, a promise rings,
The light within, it never stings.

With every storm, my fire renews,
A phoenix rising, skies of blues,
For spirit's blaze, forever bright,
Shall pierce the dark, transform the night.

In each endeavor, passion's gleam,
A spirit ablaze, life's perfect scheme,
From embers small to roaring flame,
In fiery heart, I carve my name.

Milton Keynes UK
Ingram Content Group UK Ltd.
UKHW020330050824
446478UK00015B/497